T0344187

EFFICIENT MARKING

EFFICIENT
MARKING

{ Claire Gadsby }

SAGE Publications Ltd
1 Oliver's Yard
55 City Road
London EC1Y 1SP

CORWIN
A SAGE company
2455 Teller Road
Thousand Oaks, California 91320
(0800)233-9936
www.corwin.com

SAGE Publications India Pvt Ltd
B 1/I 1 Mohan Cooperative Industrial Area
Mathura Road
New Delhi 110 044

SAGE Publications Asia-Pacific Pte Ltd
3 Church Street
#10-04 Samsung Hub
Singapore 049483

Editor: Delayna Spencer
Senior assistant editor: Catriona McMullen
Production editor: Tanya Szwarnowska
Copyeditor: Sharon Cawood
Proofreader: Emily Ayers
Indexer: Adam Pozner
Marketing manager: Dilhara Attygalle
Cover design: Wendy Scott
Typeset by: C&M Digitals (P) Ltd, Chennai, India

Library of Congress Control Number: 2020941171

British Library Cataloguing in Publication data

A catalogue record for this book is available from the British Library

ISBN 978-1-5297-3045-6 (pbk)

For my lovely family, whose support and patience enabled
me to write this book.

TABLE OF CONTENTS

[ABOUT THIS BOOK]

Marking is one of the most time-consuming and onerous of all teacher tasks. *A Little Guide for Teachers: Efficient Marking* is full of innovative and practical time-saving strategies, showing teachers how to lessen the workload whilst still moving learning forwards. The book is:

- Authored by an expert
- Easy to dip in and out of
- Full of interactive activities which encourage you to write in the book and make it your own
- Able to be read in an afternoon, or take as long as you like with it!

Find out more at
www.sagepub.co.uk/littleguides

[ABOUT THE SERIES]

A LITTLE GUIDE FOR TEACHERS series is little in size but big on all the support and inspiration you need to navigate your day-to-day life as a teacher.

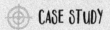 CASE STUDY

 HINTS & TIPS

 REFLECTION

 RESOURCES

 NOTE THIS DOWN

ABOUT THE AUTHOR

Author of the widely selling book, *The Perfect Assessment for Learning* (Independent Thinking Press, 2012), Claire Gadsby is an educational consultant, trainer and keynote speaker with more than 20 years of experience in education, and who has worked with hundreds of schools in the UK and overseas to raise achievement.

Claire believes passionately in 'walking the talk', and regularly coaches teachers in the classroom to demonstrate innovative pedagogies. A leading expert on formative assessment, time-efficient feedback and literacy and reading, Claire strives to improve outcomes for all pupils and to help teachers to work smarter, not harder.

www.clairegadsby.com

@greatergadsby

INTRODUCTION

LESS OF THE SUNDAY NIGHT BLUES

I genuinely believe that teaching is the greatest job in the world but it is far from an easy one. According to the Department for Education's 2014 Workload Challenge, a consultation which gathered more than 44,000 responses from teachers and support staff, marking was identified as the single biggest contributor to unsustainable workload (Elliott et al., 2016). So, it comes down to this: how to thrive, rather than merely survive, as a teacher but without becoming burnt out and disillusioned by the marking burden?

 REFLECTION

Identify your default thinking. When you hear the word 'marking', what are the first three words or thoughts that pop into your head? Make a note here:

....

....

....

The fact remains that marking is synonymous with teaching. Indeed, if I asked you to list three objects commonly associated with teachers, I can guarantee that a red pen would feature high on the list – right up there with coffee and whiteboards. However, in a changing and more evidence-informed profession, now is the ideal time to consider why we mark pupils' work and how we can do this most effectively.

DO WE NEED SAVING FROM OURSELVES?

Perverse as it may sound, I wonder sometimes if we are our own worst enemies: conscientious, committed to our pupils and always willing to go the extra mile – but at what personal cost? Like me, many of you may have used the Covid-19 pandemic as an enforced opportunity to reflect upon and reassess your priorities. One of its biggest lessons must surely be that life is short and people are precious. If you are wanting to recalibrate your work–life balance – and to claw back more time for the things that really matter to you – then this book is for you.

One of the first things to acknowledge is that much of our practice as teachers stems from habit rather than conscious choice. This is particularly true when it comes to marking and feedback: there is often a very real sense of 'this is just what I've always done'. Throughout this book, I will be encouraging you to explore your 'default' thinking and behaviours and to consider whether there might be a better alternative.

A word of warning in advance: I will ask you to consider stopping some of the things you are currently doing, and I know from experience that some of you may find this difficult. I have had the privilege of working with tens of thousands of teachers in my role as a consultant and I am continually struck by how willing teachers are to take on extra, new responsibilities and tasks – but how reluctant we are to relinquish any.

PROBLEMS WITH MARKING

Take a look at the list below. How many of these potential pitfalls of marking resonate with you? Which would you rank as the top three?

- Hugely time-consuming for busy teachers

- Not valued by pupils

- Pupils cannot understand it

- Pupils unable to respond to it independently and effectively

- Comments tend to be repetitive

- Fails to secure lasting improvements – pupils repeat the same mistakes in the future.

We now know that much feedback is flawed and, depressingly, leading assessment expert Professor Dylan Wiliam claims that feedback can actually make pupils' work worse' (Kluger and DeNisi, 1996).

Therefore, this book will focus on two key priorities:

1. Providing busy teachers with effective and time-efficient strategies for producing meaningful feedback. As Dylan Wiliam famously notes, 'Feedback should be more work for the recipient than the donor' (2011: 132).

2. Providing feedback which serves as an empowerment tool for pupils and generates improvements that last far beyond the immediate task.

HOW CAN WE MAKE OUR MARKING (FEEDBACK) MORE EFFECTIVE? TOP TAKE-AWAYS FROM THE RESEARCH

*   It is important that busy teachers devote their time to things that are proven to make the most difference. According to John Hattie's *Visible Learning for Teachers* (2011), feedback is in the top 10 influences on pupils' achievement and has a huge positive effect size of 0.7.

*   Marking (feedback) does not exist in a vacuum and is only one important element of formative assessment, the others being:

    a. Sharing learning intentions

    b. Effective questioning and discussion

    c. Activating pupils as owners of their own learning

    d. Activating pupils as resources for each other (Leahy, Lyon, Thompson and Wiliam, 2005).

As teachers, we need to ensure that all of these aspects are working together in our classroom if feedback is to be optimised.

*   Feedback should improve the person and not just the work. The best feedback will link to growth mindsets and have a longevity with its legacy extending beyond the current piece of work (Dylan Wiliam on Twitter, 28 March 2018).

According to John Hattie (cited in Sutton et al., 2011):

- Feedback should focus on the task not the learner

- Feedback should be as clear and specific as possible

- Feedback should promote a learning goal orientation via feedback

- Disconfirmation is more powerful than confirmation. Pupils need to see and accept where they have made mistakes.

GETTING STARTED: FIRM FOUNDATIONS IN YOUR CLASSROOM

The pressures on today's young people are well documented, with many experts warning of a genuine mental health crisis. Therefore, I think it is critically important that we adopt the doctor's oath: do no harm. Real damage can be done when we get feedback wrong. For some pupils, critique can feel dangerously close to judgement and threat, unless we have invested in a classroom culture that is supportive and where feedback is recognised as being central to everyone's success.

Effective feedback is dependent upon positive relationships and a culture of trust and respect between teacher and pupils – and between the pupils themselves. Only in such an environment can feedback truly flourish and be received and welcomed.

England Rugby coach Eddie Jones is famous for his blunt but highly effective feedback to his players, and at the heart of this is what he calls 'performance relationships' (see www.uppingyourelvis.com/article/emulating-the-eddie-jones-england-rugby-leadership-style) – in other words, the ability to have robust, honest conversations that are all about improving performance and not in any way personal. This is the culture we need to strive for in our classrooms. To borrow Ron Berger's (2003) famous phrase, we need to 'be kind, be specific, be helpful' (p. 93).

CHAPTER 1
DO YOU NEED TO TAKE THE MARKING HOME?

This chapter will equip you with techniques for:

- Tackling marking within school
- Involving pupils more actively in the marking process
- Making the best use of your time.

CASE STUDY

A REFLECTION FROM MY OWN LIFE

Remember that you are only human. An extended period of illness very nearly finished my teaching career in its infancy. What that frightening time in my own life created was a period of enforced reflection which led to the realisation that, in order to keep teaching, I would need to work differently. Since then I have focused on conserving the dynamic best of my energy for the classroom by learning how to deal with marking and other tasks in a more efficient way.

WORKLOAD AND WELLBEING

Teachers are busy people. In every minute of every day, they are juggling multiple and competing priorities. There is always another resource to differentiate, a lesson to plan or a child who needs extra support. You will never find a teacher who has nothing to do!

Undoubtedly, there is a buzz that comes from busyness and many teachers thrive on this energy; however, teacher workload and wellbeing remain a concern. According to the DfE's workload review:

> most respondents said they still felt they spent too much time on planning, marking, data management and general administrative work. In addition, about seven out of ten primary respondents and nine out of ten secondary respondents still report that workload is a 'fairly' or 'very serious' problem. The findings suggest there is further work to do in reducing the amount of time teachers, middle leaders and senior leaders spend on these non-teaching activities.
> (Walker et al., 2019: 11)

Marking is one of the most labour-intensive of these non-teaching activities and, according to the Report of the Independent Teacher Workload Review Group (Independent Teacher Workload Review Group (ITWRG), 2016: 5), 'providing *written* feedback on pupils' work – has become disproportionately valued by schools and has become unnecessarily burdensome for teachers.'

 ## REFLECTION

How much of an impact does marking currently have on your work–life balance and sense of wellbeing? Make a mark on the continuum below:

1 (very little) ·· **10 (huge impact)**

Make a list of the specific ways in which marking encroaches on your life outside of school:

....

....

....

....

....

How willing do you feel you are to improve this by making changes to your practice?

1 (unwilling to change) ············· **10 (totally motivated to change)**

Ultimately, teachers need to save the best of their finite human energy for the moment when they step into the classroom and begin to bring the curriculum to life for the young people that they teach. To do this, they need restorative rest at home in the evenings and certainly during weekends and holidays. To put it simply – too many brilliant teachers are suffering from burnout because they are spending too much time on tasks like marking. So, what if we were to stop taking marking home?

This chapter will explore how feedback and marking can be dealt with within the school day and within lessons. Not only is this particularly useful in supporting teachers to maintain more of a work–life balance, it also helps to ensure that feedback has far greater immediacy and impact on pupils' learning.

NOT ALL WORK IS THE SAME

Dylan Wiliam (cited in Hendrick and Macpherson, 2017) recommends 'four quarters' feedback', whereby:

- 25% of work is marked in detail by the teacher

- 25% is skim-marked by the teacher

- 25% is marked by peers

- 25% is self-marked.

This formula alone can be very liberating for teachers, freeing them from the expectation that every piece of work in every pupil's book must be marked. It reminds us that some work is, by its nature, more complex or important and necessitates thorough marking, whilst other tasks may require far less attention.

The other key implication here is that, with appropriate support, pupils can be empowered to play a much more active role in the assessment process, as we will explore in Chapter 2.

*'Take rest; a field that has rested
gives a bountiful crop.'*
Ovid

HINTS & TIPS

Do not focus on the deficit idea of what you are not doing for your pupils (e.g. sitting up until midnight writing in every book), but instead on what you are providing by changing your practice: even more engaging lessons because you are less tired, plus a genuine opportunity to become fully involved in the assessment process through the mechanisms of peer and self-assessment. Remember that more than anything else, your pupils need and deserve you at your brilliant best in the classroom. They get one go at each academic year and it is in your hands to make it as good as possible.

CLASSROOM STRATEGIES

- **'A tick and a flick'** – as previously noted, not all work needs to be marked in detail by the teacher. Some work requires little more than a tick to acknowledge it and a quick flick through the book. The purpose of this kind of marking is a simple quality assurance check: has the work been completed? Is there sufficient quantity and at the expected standard? Does this pupil appear to be taking their learning seriously and following the school's presentation protocols? This is a low-effort activity for teachers but helps to reassure pupils (as well as parents and other stakeholders) that you are aware of what pupils are doing and that you acknowledge their efforts.

- **Entrances and exits** to lessons are a great opportunity to provide the quick 'tick and a flick' type of feedback described above. Invite pupils to wait outside of the classroom with their books/work open and ready to show you. As pupils pass by you to enter the classroom, greet them whilst scanning their work. Quickly add a tick (or similar) to each child's work and keep track of pupils who may need a follow-up of any kind. You are likely to find yourself automatically adding verbal feedback as well, and this sort of personalised acknowledgement at the start of the lesson really helps to establish high expectations for the whole lesson. This strategy works particularly well for checking homework.

- **Random checks** within the lesson can be very easily generated and managed by the teacher. For example, 'Pupils with birthdays in January or May, please bring your book to me now'. The randomised element is engaging for pupils and serves to remind all pupils that their work could be selected at any time.

- **Sample marking** – you do not always need to look at every book to be able to provide useful feedback. You might decide to quickly look at 6–8 books (drawn from across the class's ability range) over lunch or break time in order to draw out common issues that can then be explored with the whole class, even later that same day , e.g. 'When I looked at your books over lunchtime, I noticed that a lot of you were struggling with X .... Now check whether you are doing the same in your work'.

 ## CASE STUDY

LESSONS FROM INDUSTRY: POMODORO MARKING

Lee, a secondary history teacher, was very struck by how productive his wife, a project manager, was whenever she was working. When he asked her about this, she introduced him to a productivity strategy called the Pomodoro technique (see https://francescocirillo.com/pages/pomodoro-technique) and explained that she had been using this for several months. The strategy, which takes its name from the tasty, bite-sized tomato, simply involves setting a timer for 25 minutes and endeavouring to tackle as much as you can during that time but, crucially, without the pressure or expectation of finishing a particular task.

Lee decided to trial this approach to tackle his marking which, in his words, often felt like 'an insurmountable task' that was taking up all of his time.

What Lee said:

> I really wanted my weekends back and decided to
> see if I could get the marking done at school instead.
> I experimented by trying to find 25 minutes within the
> school day, usually at lunchtime or during a free period.
> When I couldn't manage that, a maximum of 25 minutes
> didn't feel too daunting to tack onto the end of the day. I
> gave myself permission to only mark as many books as I
> could within that time limit: as soon as the timer beeped
> after 25 minutes, I stopped.
>
> I used my observations and notes from these books to
> give generalised feedback to the rest of the class next
> lesson, making sure that the pupils whose books had
> not been marked were the ones I started with next
> time. On another occasion, I marked the remaining
> books with the pupils in class next lesson and that also
> worked well.
>
> Trust me, you really should try the Pomodoro approach for
> your marking. You will be amazed by just how much you
> can achieve in 25 minutes when this is your sole focus.

- **Live marking** involves the teacher modelling the marking process live in front of the class. The most important element here is for the teacher to verbalise the thinking behind the marking, e.g. 'So, I am putting a tick here because ...' or 'I can see that this person has picked up their third point from the mark scheme because ... so they are now on 3 marks out of 4'. Following this, the pupils copy what the teacher has just done by applying the pointers to their work: 'Can you see any of this in your/your partner's work?'.

- **Uplevelling** – focus your energy on modelling for the pupils exactly how to edit and improve their own work by doing exactly this to sample pieces of work that you have looked at. The key here is to talk as you work so that pupils can see exactly what you are doing and hear why, e.g. 'So, I notice here that we are missing a connective to link the ideas so I am going to add the word "therefore" and then I can extend that sentence a bit more ....' or ' The first thing I notice here is that the axes have been draw without a ruler and that the scale is not accurate. I'm going to correct that first of all ...'.

Interactive whiteboards or visualisers are ideal for this, but you can achieve the same effect by taking a photo of the work and projecting this onto any kind of screen.

Here, pupils have the opportunity to stop you at any point and to ask for clarification – something that cannot be achieved through traditional written feedback.

Next, urge pupils to replicate the process and to improve their own work by making similar changes to the ones you made. Keep the exemplars displayed on the board to continue to support and scaffold the pupils, thus freeing you up to work directly with any pupils who would benefit from further guidance.

- **Cluster marking** – invite pupils to join you for specific feedback and input in relation to just one particular aspect, e.g. 'I am now going to look again at how we use evidence from the text to support our argument. If you would like some feedback on that aspect, meet me around this table now'. This approach has the added benefit of encouraging pupils to take more active ownership and responsibility within the feedback process, a principle that we will explore more fully in Chapter 2.

In summary, the Teacher Workload Survey (Walker et al., 2019) concluded that 'three principles underpin effective marking: it should be meaningful, manageable and motivating' (p.8).

The tried-and-tested strategies in this chapter will undoubtedly help to make marking more manageable. If we agree with Sir John Jones that teachers are the 'magic-weaving profession' (Jones, 2011), we need to help them to conserve their best energy for the classroom and, in some cases, to save them from their own current habits that simply may not be sustainable in the long term.

NOTE IT DOWN

How could you make this work for you? Have a think about your working week in school. What slots exist within your timetable that could be used to incorporate some of the strategies listed in this chapter?
Label the slots:

- Possible

- Probable

- Preferred.

OVER A TYPICAL WEEK, TRY TO SEE IF YOU CAN TRIAL SOME
NEW APPROACHES IN YOUR PREFERRED SLOTS. WHAT IMPACT
DO YOU NOTICE ON YOUR WORK–LIFE BALANCE AND LEISURE
TIME OUTSIDE OF SCHOOL?

Table 1.1   Ideas for new approaches to work–life balance

	Before school	Morning break	Lunchtime	Immediately after school	Other, e.g. free period
Monday					
Tuesday					
Wednesday					
Thursday					
Friday					

CHAPTER 2
DO YOU NEED TO WRITE IN EVERY BOOK?

This chapter encourages you to think about:

- The problems with written feedback
- Myths around marking
- How codes and symbols allow every pupil to access the marking.

'I once estimated that if you priced teachers' time appropriately, in England we spend about two and a half billion pounds a year on feedback – and it has almost no effect on student achievement.'
Dylan Wiliam Cited in Hendricks

THE PROBLEM WITH WRITING

It may surprise you to learn that, according to the Education Endowment Fund (Elliott et al., 2016), there is relatively little robust and large-scale research evidence to attest to the impact of written feedback – and yet the prevalence of written feedback persists across the profession. Although teachers spend many hours generating written feedback for their pupils, the depressing reality is that many pupils either cannot read or accurately understand what is meant by it. This problem of access is further compounded for very young children and those pupils with SEND.

 REFLECTION

Another key challenge is pupils' willingness to engage with – and actively respond to – feedback.

Pupils need time to respond to feedback. This is often referred to as DIRT (dedicated improvement and reflection time) (Beere, 2012):

- **Do you regularly allocate time for this?**

- **How effectively are your pupils utilising this time?**

I describe our current generation of technologically savvy young people as the 'instant gratification' generation: constantly clicking and swiping and used to instantaneous responses from their technology. For these pupils, written feedback – often provided days after the work has been submitted – must seem particularly obsolete and outdated. They may feel that the work is finished and that feedback after the fact is pointless. The best feedback needs to challenge this idea and entice them to return to the business of editing and improving their work.

Essentially, we can measure the efficacy of our current feedback by observing how much editing and improving the pupils are able to do *without* our support. Ideally, the feedback should be unambiguous, meaning that pupils can tackle the improvement tasks without asking questions of their teacher.

SO, WHAT IF WE TAKE AWAY THE WRITING?

I have been fascinated by the extent to which the marking process is tied up with many teachers' sense of self: an entrenched and incontrovertible part of what it means to be a teacher. This is often expressed most strongly when one asks teachers to stop providing written comments. For many, there is a real sense that this would mean depriving their pupils and would somehow equate to not doing their job properly.

 HINTS & TIPS

Although this may be difficult, try not to feel guilty about work in general – and marking in particular. There is always more that could be written in a child's book, meaning that marking is a job that can never really be finished. This can feel hugely frustrating and lead to further guilt which, in turn, wears people down over time.

(Continued)

Whenever you find yourself slipping into this kind of mindset, stop what you are doing and consciously shift your focus away from what you 'ought' to have done and focus instead on three things you have done brilliantly for your pupils recently. Plurals are powerful and reiterating the three positives (perhaps that great resource you created or the way you drew a hesitant pupil into a discussion) will create a more positive perspective on your work.

Interestingly, some of the most exciting and effective feedback I have seen in recent years does not involve any writing at all. Instead, teachers have been using codes, symbols and annotated copies of the original success criteria to provide highly effective feedback without any harm being done to the pupils! Indeed, an added benefit is that these approaches also generate meaningful improvement tasks that pupils can access independently, during DIRT time.

STRATEGIES FOR THE CLASSROOM

- **Single-colour highlighting** – having a clear set of agreed success criteria (see Chapter 5) will make feedback easier to generate for the teacher and be more accessible to the pupils – what we might call a win-win situation. Assuming that you have established a maximum of six success criteria in a numbered grid format, you can quickly and easily mark a pupil's work simply by highlighting up to two numbers on their copy of the grid. These will serve as pupils' feedback and development points.

  Resist the temptation to highlight the whole success criteria; you will achieve the same effect by simply highlighting the number itself.

  Although many schools have developed systems where staff use two coloured highlighters, I would argue that this is twice the effort and is unnecessary. What we want to achieve is feedback which is as clear as possible for pupils to decipher and I find that this is best achieved by using just one colour. If a particular criterion is not highlighted, then it does not require attention from the pupil.

When providing feedback by highlighting the grid, differentiation can be achieved in a variety of ways, such as:

o   Challenging pupils to find where they have left out the success criteria

o   Highlighting in the margin close to where the error can be found

o   Directly pointing out where the criteria have been missed.

- **Silver star** – the single-colour highlighting strategy described above can be enhanced by introducing a silver star sticker (or any other positive symbol or mark of your choice). Place the silver star next to the criterion which has been met most successfully – the pupil's stand-out achievement. This allows teachers to celebrate the aspect they have done best in and effectively replaces the rather ubiquitous 'Well done' comment.

  An important by-product of this approach is the fact that you can then group pupils in such a way that they can help each other, e.g. 'If you got a silver star for criterion 1, come and sit at this table. You are now the experts or ambassadors for number 1. Anyone who received number 1 as a highlighted target for improvement, you will need to visit table 1 and talk to these people and look at their work'. This is another great way to encourage collaboration and peer and self-assessment (see Chapter 2).

- **Symbols** are quicker to generate than words and, once established, more easily understood by pupils. Many schools already use a range of symbols in their marking, often to denote grammatical or spelling issues, e.g. P – new paragraph needed; A – capital letter needed.

  However, these symbols are often used as well as – rather than instead of – written comments. Consider whether the range of symbols could be expanded, thereby negating the need for any written comments at all.

It is reassuring to note that research suggests there is no difference between the effectiveness of coded or un-coded feedback, providing that pupils understand what the codes mean (Elliott et al., 2016).

 ## CASE STUDY

GO BACK TO THE GRID

Teachers at Priestmead Primary School worked with me to explore ways of marking in a more manageable and effective way. One of their frustrations occurred as they found themselves writing the same comment repeatedly in different pupils' books. Instead, they adopted the principle of writing each comment only once but in a format that could be shared with every child simultaneously. They achieved this by going back to the original success criteria grid (see Chapter 5) and recording the comments there.

As staff became more comfortable with this new approach, and saw how well pupils were responding, they began to adapt the original success criteria grid to also include specific instructions for the DIRT tasks they wanted pupils to complete. In the two examples below, the teacher used purple text (lightly highlighted in Figure 2.1) to provide pupils with sentence stems to help them to complete their improvement tasks independently.

What the teachers said:

> **As the marking does not take as long, the focus shifts to thinking of tasks and other ways to bridge the gaps in pupils' understanding.**

> **We use WN (What Next) on a class-to-class basis and these will depend on the understanding of the lesson. It feels good to know that we are putting our energy into the most useful actions to help our pupils.**

EXAMPLE 1

1.	Finish describing each of the seasons in your book.	 • Spring • Summer • Autumn • Winter
2.	Explain the climate at the equator and the polar regions.	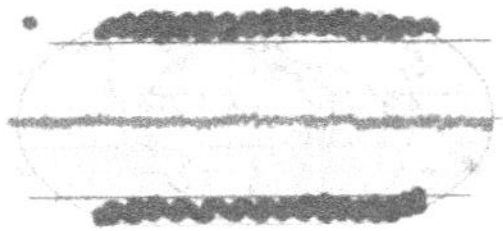
3.	How could the weather change daily in the season of autumn? During autumn, the weather in a day could go from. . . The temperature would be coldest in _____ and warmest at _____ because . . .	
4.	Explain the climate in the sub-tropics and the temperate regions.	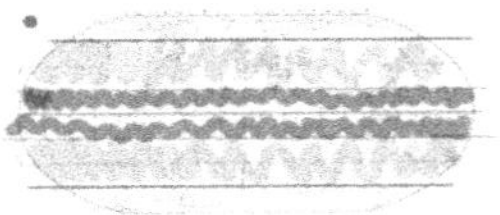
5.	I want to go to the rainforest on holiday. What would you recommend I take with me and why? If you are going to the rainforest I recommend . . . because	

If all green OR you have finished your first WN, get WN 1 from the front.

Figure 2.1 Amending the original grid to provide feedback – example 1

EXAMPLE 2

LO	To write a movie review			
1.	I can include a summary of the film	Beginning	Middle	End
		Key events		
2.	I can include opinions about the film	Film magazine has been quoted saying that this is the funniest children's film of the year so far!			
3.	I can include key features of a review	Headings	sub-headings	key factors and figures	
4.	I can use a range of co-ordinating and subordinating conjunctions	and	They travelled to the kingdom of Far Far Away in an onion carriage and they did not enjoy the long journey.		
		Or	They could remain as humans, or they could return to being ogres forever.		
		but	Princess Fiona was excited to visit her parents but Shrek felt the opposite.		
		When	When they arrived in the Kingdom of Far Far Away, they were not greeted with a warm welcome.		
		If	If Shrek had not taken the potion, he would have remained an ogre.		
		That	They drank a magic potion that turned them into humans.		
		Because	Donkey didn't want Shrek to take the potion because he was worried.		
5.	I can use a variety of punctuation	?	Who's the funniest character in the film?		
		!	What a hilarious joke that was!		
		: ;	The fairy tale features that we noticed were: Cinderalla , Gingerbread Man , Prince Charming and the three blind mice.		
		. . .	When he entered the room he did not find Princess Fiona but . . .		

Figure 2.2 Amending the original grid to provide feedback – example 2

REFLECTION

IS YOUR ATTITUDE TO SPOKEN FEEDBACK MAKING YOUR JOB MORE DIFFICULT?

Verbal feedback is possibly the most effective feedback of all because of its immediacy and the fact that it is personalised and specific. Whilst many teachers admit to feeling worried about pupils forgetting what has been said, the main concern in an accountability culture seems to be the issue of 'proof': 'How will people know what I have said?' This has led to the widespread use of stamps saying things like 'verbal feedback given'.

- How effective do you consider these kinds of stamps to be?

You can encourage far greater autonomy on the part of students by asking *them* to record what you have said in a format that will be memorable for them. You could also do this using the same grid of numbered success criteria. Here, you might ask the pupil to highlight up to two targets to develop and to silver star/code their stand-out achievement. Exactly what is highlighted should be specified by the teacher but could also incorporate targets that the pupil themselves has identified.

Not only is the process of highlighting their own grid much more memorable for the pupil but, because the teacher is standing alongside them, they can also ask for any clarification that they may need.

Finally, invite pupils to respond to your verbal feedback in the same way that they would normally respond to written feedback. You will be able to evaluate how effective your feedback is by observing how many improvements pupils are able to make

(Continued)

independently as a result. Pupils' editing is much easier to discern if they complete this using a different-coloured pen.

- **How do you feel about this approach?**
- **What benefits can you identify for both teacher and pupils?**

CRACK THE CODE MARKING

Endeavour to make the symbols as creative as possible and invite the pupils to speculate on what they might mean. For instance, 'If I have drawn a little oxygen tank by your sentence, what might that represent? Yes, you need to provide a pause to breathe. What punctuation would you need to add? Yes, a full stop. Well worked out'. Because such codes engage pupils emotionally and cognitively, they have the added advantage of being very memorable.

SECRET CODE MARKING

Begin by establishing a maximum of six success criteria with your class and ensure that each pupil has their own copy of these, presented in a numbered grid. When it comes to marking the completed work, select six different-coloured pens (I recommend bingo dabbers but any coloured pens, highlighters or even coloured stickers would suffice). These six colours will be used to represent the six success criteria but in a 'secret code' fashion that pupils will work together to decode:

- When marking the first piece of work, use your first coloured pen to make a dot. This dot represents the first success criterion that the learner has failed to achieve. Keep a key!

- Use the remaining five colours to represent the remaining success criteria. Use a different-coloured dot for each criterion that pupils have missed. You may prefer to reverse this, e.g. using the colours to denote which criteria have been achieved rather than missed. Either approach is fine if explained to the pupils.

- More than three dots for any one learner would indicate serious mis-conceptions. Make a note of the learner's name so that you can pro-vide targeted intervention during the feedback lesson.

- Build a sense of intrigue and excitement about the feedback lesson. Pupils will be quick to note that their work is not 'marked' in the usual way and will ask what the coloured dots mean. Simply tell them that it is a secret code that they must crack.

- Ensure that a version of the original six success criteria is clearly vis-ible, then invite pupils to mingle with each other and discuss which success criteria could be represented by which colour, e.g. 'We've both got orange dots – how is my work like yours? What have we both missed?' and 'You have red but not me – what's the difference?'

- Next, gather the class together and use a visualiser (or similar) to look at examples of work and to discuss their guesses regarding the colours (e.g. 'So these two pieces of work have orange dots. What is similar about them? Can you suggest which criterion orange might link to?')

- Ensure that pupils are totally clear about what the colours mean and to record this for themselves. If you have introduced the system of numbered criteria, very little needs to be recorded (e.g. orange dot = 1), clearly linking back to the success criteria grid. All of this serves to make pupil progress very transparent.

- Finally, provide ample DIRT time for pupils to tackle their targets, perhaps by colour-coding the classroom: 'If you have a purple dot, you will find your feedback task on the purple table.' Alternatively, with older pupils you may prefer a more free-form 'skill swap' ('I will show you how to improve the purple one if you can help me with green').

As the teacher, devote your energy to working with small groups of pupils who need it the most, based on this particular marking cycle. These might be those who have struggled the most and would benefit from a reteach. Alternatively, this would be an excellent opportunity to provide challenge and extension for those pupils who have excelled and who have no coloured dots on their work.

Be assured that this approach will not confuse or alienate your pupils if they have sufficient familiarity with – and access to – the success criteria.

In summary, although the idea of providing no (or even reduced) written feedback may be challenging for some teachers, this approach can represent a positive change for staff and pupils alike. The approaches suggested in this chapter have the dual advantage of being time-efficient for busy teachers, whilst making feedback more accessible to and engaging for pupils.

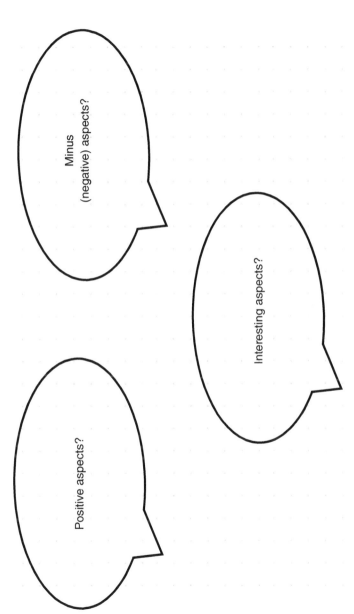

Figure 2.3 PMI thinking

NOTE IT DOWN

PMI (PLUS, MINUS, INTERESTING) THINKING IS A
REALLY USEFUL TOOL FOR EVALUATING NEW IDEAS AND
APPROACHES. USE THIS MODEL TO REFLECT ON THE
PRINCIPLE OF MARKING WITHOUT WRITING IN EVERY BOOK

CHAPTER 3
WHOSE JOB IS IT ANYWAY?

This chapter addresses:

- How self and peer assessment can ease unnecessary workload for teachers
- How we can empower pupils to be active partners in the feedback process.

In Chapter 1, I introduced the idea of four quarters' feedback (Wiliam, cited in Hendrick and Macpherson, 2017), where 50% of the marking is delegated to the pupils. I have yet to meet a teacher who would not be happy to cut their marking in half. This chapter will suggest a range of practical techniques to ensure that the feedback produced by the pupils is as good as that provided by their teachers (yes, really!).

GOOD FOR US AND GOOD FOR THEM

Perhaps the first step is to accept that pupils doing some of the marking is good for them. When we do all of the marking, we deprive pupils of several key benefits. First, as Dylan Wiliam (2011) argues, the best feedback has longevity: in other words, it should improve the person and not just the immediate piece of work. By involving pupils in self-assessment, we immerse them more fully in the processes of assessment, rendering them more meaningful and memorable over the long term.

Another key benefit is known as the hypercorrection effect: the finding that 'highly confident errors were the most likely to be corrected in a subsequent retest' ' (Butterfield and Metcalfe, 2001: 1491). In other words, pupils derive real learning from identifying and remembering the mistake they made so that they don't repeat that specific mistake again.

 REFLECTION

How comfortable do you feel about handing some of the responsibility for marking over to your pupils?

Make a note here of any benefits you can think of:

....

....

....

Now, jot down any concerns you would have:

....

....

....

Note here how you could alleviate some of these concerns:

....

....

....

So, whilst we as teachers know how important this process is, many pupils may lack the skill – and the will – to engage in self-assessment thoroughly and accurately.

 ## CASE STUDY

THE TALE OF THE FURRY PENCIL CASE: WE NEED MORE THAN FLUFFY COMMENTS ...

Picture the scene: Jenny had planned a very impressive sounding lesson which depended upon pupils providing peer feedback on each other's work. Within minutes, the lesson floundered as the majority of pupils, at a loss to know what to say, or how to say it, had wandered off topic. The only evaluative comments that remained came from one young girl who was earnestly critiquing her partner's fluffy pencil case!

(Continued)

The moral of the tale? The skills of self and peer assessment need to be prioritised, modelled and practised regularly in order to succeed in any meaningful way.

Many pupils are motivated by task completion and do not take kindly to being asked to go back to their work and check it once they think that it is finished. Instead, I recommend regular self-assessment tasks *during* ongoing work rather than waiting until the work is finished. As discussed throughout this book, having pre-agreed success criteria readily available makes this process most effective.

SELF-ASSESSMENT STRATEGIES FOR THE CLASSROOM

- **Speed read** – periodically ask pupils to pause in their work and complete a 'speed read' of what they have produced so far. The idea is that you give them a very short period of time to scan their work and see if they can spot a certain number of errors/targets to improve. I typically ask pupils to use a ruler, or other object, to help them to check their work more slowly and methodically, line by line. The timer, plus the challenge of a specific number of errors to hunt down and correct, elevates this task from the purely editorial into something more game-like and fun.

- **They mark it first** – the acronym WOMBOLL stands for 'What One of My Best Ones Looks Like'. Invite pupils to mark and annotate their own work before they hand it in to the teacher. This is most effective when done in relation to numbered success criteria (see Chapter 5). Even very young children can be encouraged to take part in this process, e.g. 'write number 1 next to your capital letter if you have used one'.

  There are many benefits to this approach. As pupils are labelling up the success criteria which they should have included, they often spot one or more that they have missed. Crucially, pupils then have the opportunity to amend their work without the teacher needing to tell them to do so, thus increasing their autonomy and metacognitive skills.

Another important benefit for the pupils is the boost they gain to their self-esteem and confidence as they are literally able to pinpoint and talk about exactly what they have done well in their work.

The gain for the teacher is equally significant because, on the same piece of work, we can see twice the evidence and type of progress: both the finished product and evidence of the thinking process behind the work – and all of this with no extra effort for the teacher!

HOW CAN PEER FEEDBACK EASE TEACHER WORKLOAD?

Peer and self-assessment are inextricably linked. Reinholz (2016) noted that through critiquing the work of their peers, pupils are exposed to a range of examples that help them to perceive degrees of quality and difference. Thus, peer assessment seems to support self-assessment by making both assessment processes more explicit.

However, as illustrated by the true story of the furry pencil case, effective peer assessment does not happen by accident or merely as a result of good intentions. In the words of John Hattie and colleagues, pupils receive a great deal of their feedback from their well-meaning peers but it is often inaccurate.

Effective self-assessment skills form the bedrock for meaningful peer assessment, and both of these rely heavily on the presence of clearly defined success criteria, as discussed in detail throughout this book. But genuine peer assessment – doing the spirit and not just the letter of the thing – requires something more.

Anyone who has watched the wonderful Ron Berger exploring peer critique with pupils in the 'Austin's Butterfly' video (see www.youtube.com/watch?v=hqh1MRWZjms) will need little persuading about the genuine power of peer-to-peer feedback. However, feedback of this kind depends upon a supportive classroom environment, a place where pupils feel safe and valued: a community of allies and not judges.

Creating this kind of ethos takes time and continued commitment from the teacher but will yield many benefits, including increased collaboration and autonomy amongst pupils. Indeed, as pupils become more confident and adept at providing this kind of feedback, they begin to regard the teacher more as a moderator and verifier of comments rather than the origin of all feedback.

PEER FEEDBACK IDEAS FOR THE CLASSROOM

'Talk as you tick' – begin by offering the board pen to a pupil and inviting them to come to the front. Explain that they will be in role as the teacher and have the responsibility for marking the model answer that is displayed on the board. Ask them to 'talk it as you tick it': explaining where they are awarding marks and why. Again, ensure that all marking links back to the agreed success criteria and always begin by using anonymous work. Invite other pupils to offer comments and suggestions.

With time and practice, you will notice that pupils are typically much more willing and comfortable to share their own work for critique and to welcome feedback as this becomes the norm.

'My turn, your turn' is a nice variation on the usual 'swap books with your partner' format for peer assessment. Ask pupils to work in pairs but to begin with one pupil reading their own work aloud before discussing it with their partner. Next, ask them to agree on some improvement targets. These should be recorded by the owner of the work (see above). Repeat the process with the second pupil's work.

As well as developing interpersonal skills and collaboration, this strategy also improves pupils' self-assessment capabilities. As pupils read their own work aloud, they often notice errors and begin to edit these independently.

ARE WE 'KILLING THEM WITH KINDNESS'?

In summary, developing pupils' self and peer assessment skills has the potential to reduce the unnecessary workload of busy teachers. We are used to bearing the burden of most, if not all, marking, and you may be feeling hesitant about handing over partial responsibility. Let us remind ourselves then that this process is hugely important for our pupils and, as noted by the Workload Review (ITWRG, 2016), whilst our detailed marking may be well-intentioned and driven by kindness, by doing too much of it we:

> detract from the challenge of a piece of work and reduce long term retention and resilience-building. Accepting work that pupils have not checked sufficiently and then providing extensive feedback detracts from pupils' responsibility for their own learning, particularly in editing and drafting skills (p.10).

NOTE IT DOWN

Take a look at the Austin's Butterfly video (www.youtube.com/watch?v=hqhiMRWZjms). As you watch, make a note of:

- The comments made by the pupils

- The comments made by the teacher

What principles for feedback strike you as being most important and transferable to your own practice?

How might you use this video clip with your class to establish expectations about peer and self-assessment?

CHAPTER 4
WHERE IS THE JOY?

This chapter covers:

- Strategies for increasing pupils' emotional engagement with feedback
- How to avoid tedium and routine when it comes to marking
- Practical suggestions for making feedback more memorable.

'Learning is the greatest game in life and the most
fun. All children are born believing this and will continue to
believe this until we convince them that learning is very
hard work and unpleasant.'
Doman and Doman, 2006: 24

BEWARE THE FORMULA

Many schools have evolved comprehensive marking policies and routines
for providing feedback. The danger here is that any routine can quickly
become formulaic and may do little to help pupils understand the relevance
of their individual feedback. Even something as important as DIRT (Dedicated
Improvement and Reflection Time, which is discussed in Chapter 3) may be
perceived by pupils as tedious and monotonous if it is always conducted in
the same way.

 REFLECTION

- How do your pupils currently feel about the feedback
  process?

- How do you know?

- What types of behaviour and comments do you
  observe when you are preparing to give back marked
  work?

- Are pupils sufficiently engaged and motivated by the
  process as well as the content of the feedback?

- **Do they care enough?**

- **Do you ever feel that your role in the feedback process has become formulaic and 'flat'?**

This chapter will equip teachers with a range of ideas for boosting pupils' emotional engagement with feedback. Let us be clear from the outset: this is not just fluffy, feel-good stuff. Research has shown that emotional engagement is associated with positive outcomes for student success, including academic achievement (Bulger et al., 2008).

Beyond this, we also need feedback to be highly memorable for our pupils if it is to have relevance beyond just the immediate piece of work, and we can support memory by heightening emotional involvement. An article published in 2017, reviewing neuroscientific studies on the impact of emotion on learning, suggests that emotionally stimulating events are remembered more clearly, accurately and for longer periods of time than emotionally neutral events (Tyng et al., 2017).

 # REFLECTION

It is estimated that an average teacher will deliver approximately 22,500 lessons in a 20-year career. Take a moment to think about the aspects of the job that bring you the most joy and satisfaction. When are you at your happiest as a teacher? Which aspects of teaching may have become formulaic and less satisfying?

So, the key here lies in helping pupils to care more about feedback than they did previously: let's get our pupils feeling intrigued, empowered and motivated when it comes to all types of feedback.

Whilst preparation will be needed in advance of these lessons, trust me when I say that the time invested will be more than rewarded when you get to witness the pupils' responses to the kind of feedback activities suggested below.

STRATEGIES FOR THE CLASSROOM

- **Find your feedback** – start the feedback session by giving pupils back their unmarked work (note: you will have looked at each pupil's work in advance of this lesson but, rather than writing anything in their book, you will simply have written down their name up to a maximum of twice next to a specific success criterion). Explain that the challenge for the pupils will be to correctly 'find their own feedback'.

  o   Begin by displaying an anonymous exemplar and live-mark it, talking as you do. Be sure to draw out the specific common feedback points (in other words, the comments that you would normally have found yourself writing over and over again in the books!) and ensure that this continues to refer back to the pre-agreed success criteria.

  o   Once this is completed, display large copies of these comments around the room, e.g. 'Expand your point by referring to another linked character or theme in the text' or 'Plot the co-ordinates neatly on the line'. Ensure that each child's name appears on a sticky note on the back of at least one of the comments. Next, invite pupils to move around and view all of the comments and to guess which of them will have their name concealed on the back, e.g. 'Ryan, can you guess what I said about your work?'

  o   Then, ask pupils to stand next to their chosen comment and, on the count of three, ask them to turn the paper over to see whether or not they were correct. If you are lucky enough to have a pupil suggest that they had guessed a different comment than the one you provided, invite them to adopt their own target as well as yours.

  o   During the final phase of this feedback session, invite the pupils with the same target (and their names on the same sticky note) to work together to improve that aspect of their work. As the teacher, you can support the specific groups in turn. Don't forget to keep referring pupils back to the exemplar which you critiqued on the board at the start of the session.

CASE STUDY

FEEDBACK AS A TEAM CHALLENGE

What Ben (12) said:

Being honest, it is usually pretty boring when we have to do improvements on our work. Today's lesson was much better because we got to do it as a challenge in groups. The teacher looked at our books but didn't write in them. Instead, Miss gave each group a sheet of paper that was like a quiz. There were some missing words and pictures or clues.

We had a competition to see which group could figure out what the feedback meant first. It was fun and our group came second. Afterwards, we had to check through our work carefully to see what changes we could make based on the feedback sheet. It was cool because the people in our group all helped each other.

What the teacher said:

I loved this lesson! The pupils really came to life when I explained that feedback would be a competition. It was great to see the pupils working together and getting excited about something like feedback. This has never happened before!

I think that the collaborative and competitive elements will help to make the feedback messages more memorable.

Next time, I am going to make the challenge different by giving each group their feedback sheet chopped up and

(Continued)

needing to be sequenced correctly in order to 'unlock' the hidden messages.

Most of all, I liked the fact that, because I wasn't spending hours writing in everybody's book, I had the time to think about how to make the feedback lesson so much better.

- **'Mystery text' marking** – is a fabulous strategy for encouraging really close listening. I use it regularly in day-to-day teaching when introducing new text extracts or other key information to pupils. In short, the teacher holds the only copy of the text and reads this to the pupils three times. During each reading, pupils can only listen but, as soon as the teacher stops speaking, their challenge is to write down as much as they can remember. This can be done individually or in groups and is highly engaging on a pedagogical level.

  - The approach works equally well when applied to the feedback process. Begin by reading the pupils' work as usual (or you may choose to just focus on a carefully selected sample) and make a note of the common errors and targets for improvement. As discussed throughout this book, try to relate these as closely as possible to the pre-agreed success criteria. Next, share these with the class, using the sequence described above.

  - Typically, you will notice pupils concentrating very attentively on what the teacher says – and with the added benefit that they hear this repeated three times and must personally record it. Encourage pupils to compare their notes before displaying your original text. Now, invite pupils to scrutinise their work in light of the common targets and to make at least two improvements or additions. It is much easier to spot these if pupils do their amendments in a different colour.

- **Just-a-peek feedback** – in common with the mystery text-marking approach described above, the idea is that the teacher reads the work and records common errors and targets in advance of the lesson. These are then summarised on a large piece of paper in the most concise but memorable way possible. I find that picture or symbol clues work particularly well as they encourage pupils to decode and problem-solve.

o   Arrange pupils into groups of up to four and ask them to number themselves. Next, give each group a large piece of paper and marker pens and explain that this feedback will take place in the form of a group challenge to recreate most accurately, and then interpret, the feedback messages shown on your secret sheet. Using the numbers, invite one person from each team to come and look at your 'secret sheet' and go back and record on their team's sheet. Continue until all members of the team have taken a turn. Ask pupils to compare their version before revealing the original sheet for comparison. Finally, invite pupils to edit and improve their own work, paying particular attention to the messages on the sheet.

o   This approach is hugely engaging, and the competitive, playful energy helps to enhance the feedback messages. Pupils remember what we tell them in part because of how we tell them and how this makes them feel.

- **Mix-and-match feedback** – read pupils' work and collate the main recommendations. Keep these as brief as possible. Next, for each common target/area for development, generate one brief example. Ensure that these are not drawn directly from any one pupil's work but rather are an amalgamation from several pupils or, better still, an example you have created yourself.

o   Next, display the targets and examples in a randomised way. This could be done on one sheet of paper (draw a line to match the target and the example) or cut up ready for physically matching. Ask pupils to work in pairs to correctly match the targets and examples. This activity can also be extended by adding a third component: an example of each area/aspect done brilliantly well.

In summary, if we are going to make the effort to provide feedback, it makes sense to think about how we can deliver it in such a way as to make it more memorable for the pupils, and more joyful for both them and us.

NOTE IT DOWN

CAST YOUR MIND BACK AND THINK ABOUT ONE OF THE MOST ENGAGING AND SUCCESSFUL LESSONS YOU HAVE EVER TAUGHT.

WHAT MADE THE LESSON SO SUCCESSFUL?

WHAT WERE YOU DOING?

WHAT WERE THE PUPILS DOING?

WHAT ELEMENTS FROM THIS LESSON COULD YOU ADAPT AND APPLY IN ORDER TO MAKE FEEDBACK MORE ENGAGING?

CHAPTER 5

HOW CAN SUCCESS CRITERIA MAKE MARKING EASIER AND MORE EFFECTIVE?

This chapter covers:

- Why success criteria are so important when it comes to marking
- The practicalities of success criteria – how many and how often?
- How to engage all pupils more fully in using success criteria.

> *'Most students can hit the target if they*
> *can see it clearly and it stays still.'*
> Rick Stiggins, 2004: 57

THE REALITY OF THE JOB

Tell me: does the following scenario sound familiar? You have taught a particular topic with great energy. The pupils have responded positively and have tackled the work set with enthusiasm. Later, you settle down to mark their work, feeling optimistic and already anticipating the high calibre of work you are going to see. However, upon opening the first few books, your optimism disappears as you are confronted with work that is, at least in part, disappointing.

 ## REFLECTION

Have you experienced something similar to the opening scenario?

What did you feel at that time?

How motivated were you to continue with the whole pile of marking?

How did this affect your motivation and confidence when it came to setting the next piece of work?

Somewhere, between the teacher's input and the finished work, misconceptions can and do occur. How, then, can we ensure that the expectations we have for pupils' work are internalised and fully understood by all pupils? Is there a shared language and understanding of what 'good' looks like?

SUCCESS CRITERIA: THE BUSY TEACHER'S BEST FRIEND

Success criteria, also commonly known as steps to success, are crucial and can be defined as the precise requirements for a piece of work broken down into increments or steps for pupils to follow. I often describe success criteria as the poor relation when it comes to formative assessment: rather under-appreciated but with magical, transformative potential to improve the quality of pupils' work. This chapter will show you how to actively involve pupils in the co-construction of success criteria and how these can then be used to provide highly focused and meaningful feedback.

Whilst success criteria play an important role in supporting pupil progress, such progress is not guaranteed simply by providing pupils with a pre-prepared checklist of success criteria. Many well-intentioned and busy teachers do provide exactly these sorts of lists in the hope that pupils will refer to them and then include the features in their own work: if only it were that simple!

Whilst many teachers often share mark schemes with their pupils, many pupils struggle to access such rubrics because, by their very nature, these are designed for use by teachers and are loaded with jargon. The challenge lies in helping pupils to engage more fully with the idea of what great work actually looks and feels like: 'Pupils should be taught and encouraged to check their own work by understanding the success criteria, presented in an age appropriate way, so that they complete work to the highest standard' (ITWRG, 2016: 10).

 ## REFLECTION

Co-constructing the success criteria with the pupils is a powerful way of helping pupils to fully internalise and 'own' these features.

(Continued)

Let's explore how this could look for you by thinking of a particular piece of work you might set. Highlight which of the following approaches would work best for you and your pupils:

1.   Give pupils a selection of sample answers/models/finished products to explore and critique. Challenge them to identify six things that made them good.

2.   Provide pupils with a selection of possible success criteria, some of which are correct features and some of which are not. Ask them to identify which are which.

3.   Give pupils eight success criteria and challenge them to identify the six most important. Next, they should rank-order these in terms of importance or difficulty. Explore which two have been rejected by the pupils and why.

4.   Can you think of another idea?

HOW CAN WE ENSURE THAT PUPILS ARE SUFFICIENTLY ENGAGED BY, AND CONVERSANT WITH, THE SUCCESS CRITERIA?

Having too many criteria within one piece of work can be unwieldy for pupils and may ultimately make work less successful. I recommend six or fewer criteria, and the challenge for the teacher is to identify and then foreground precisely which are the six most important components that will form these criteria.

The challenge then is to keep the success criteria at the very forefront of day-to-day learning by challenging pupils to recall them from memory or perhaps to spot the 'odd one out' in an adapted version. The aim is to develop pupils' knowledge of the criteria to such an extent that they are able to incorporate them into their own work automatically and with increasing fluency and skill.

During independent work, build in plenty of opportunities for pupils to self and peer assess against the success criteria which will further increase their familiarity with the expectations (see Chapter 3).

In my work with hundreds of schools each year, I have found the following strategies to work particularly well with pupils of all ages and in all subject areas. Note that when I talk about providing examples of work for exploration and critique at this stage, ideally this should not be pupil work from your current class. I recommend using anonymous examples and often create substandard model answers myself, incorporating real phrases or common misconceptions drawn from the work of different pupils. Keeping hold of pupil work from previous classes will provide you with useful resources for the future.

The huge potential of peer and self-assessment is explored in Chapter 3 but it is really important that no child feels singled out for a negative reason.

STRATEGIES FOR THE CLASSROOM

- **A 'good or a dud?'** – provide pupils with two specimen answers, one of which should be a good exemplar and the other a substandard ('dud') one. Challenge them to identify which is which and to explain their thinking. Invite them to label six features that appeared in the good example and explain that these are the success criteria you will be asking them to include in their own work.

- **'Turn a dud one into a good one'** – once pupils have identified that an exemplar is a 'dud' (substandard) example, challenge them to make six changes that could improve it. These six changes will then form the success criteria for their own work.

- **Dual coding** – first described by Allan Paivio in 1971, dual coding theory is a theory of cognition and how we think. Central to dual coding theory is the idea that the formation of mental images supports learning and memory. Wherever possible, I would urge you to provide pictures or symbols alongside the written success criteria, thereby rendering them twice as effective and memorable (see Figure 2.1 in Chapter 2). Even better, invite the pupils themselves to create – or select – their own images if they are able to do so.

- **See it, say it, do it!** The gold standard for me would be for pupils to then perform a simple action to go with each criterion: triple coding if you will! Not only is this great fun but it also serves to activate muscle memory. Pupils themselves are very intuitive about what actions to use in order to remember certain criteria, e.g. interlocking thumbs and forefingers to signify conjunctions or weighing with two hands to show evaluation. Crucially, if pupils struggle here – or suggest vague actions – teachers can intervene to address any misconceptions immediately.

These kinds of approaches can be employed creatively with pupils from reception right through to year 13 in order to increase engagement with – and understanding of – the success criteria.

Once you have established the success criteria, the following techniques are useful in keeping the success criteria in constant use:

- Present the agreed success criteria but with omissions. Can you remember what the second one should say?

- Present just the pictures and challenge pupils to recall the written form.

- Present the grid fleetingly, then ask pupils to work with a partner to take it in turns to say – or do the action for – one that they can remember.

- Pictionary: from memory, pupils take it in turns to draw one of the symbols and challenge their partner to recall what the corresponding written criterion was.

DISPLAYING THE SUCCESS CRITERIA TO MAKE MARKING EASY

In order to make marking as easy and effective as possible, I strongly recommend presenting the success criteria in a grid format and numbering them. Trust me when I say that the initial effort involved in establishing the criteria with the pupils will pay dividends when it comes to optimising the impact of feedback later.

HINTS & TIPS

Rather than spending hours annotating every single error in each piece of work – which can be hugely demoralising for pupils and exhausting for us as teachers – instead give yourself permission to only mark the success criteria that have been shared with the pupil. This is a much quicker and fairer process, freeing you up to focus on the evaluation of pupils' work. Which criteria have been used most successfully? Where are the misconceptions? Which criteria need to be modelled again?

CASE STUDY

SUCCESS CRITERIA BINGO!

Teachers in one of my pilot schools saw great success with this approach. They provided pupils with a blank six-box grid and announced that they were going to play a new kind of bingo. The challenge was for pupils to predict what features, or ingredients, a good piece of work would have in it before they saw it. This strategy was used with a piece of persuasive writing in English, an accurately drawn histogram and a beautifully constructed bird house. Pupils worked individually to predict six features and record them in a grid. Next, teachers revealed the exemplar work and pupils played 'bingo' by crossing off any correct guesses.

What the teachers said:

> Pupils loved this approach and it really encouraged them to look very closely at the 'good' example. There was lively debate about what constituted a correct guess. We were then able to use the resulting discussion to draw out and

(Continued)

agree on the six most important criteria that we wanted pupils to include in their work.

We were able to differentiate this easily, for example, by:

- Providing pupils with a selection of pre-prepared criteria to select from and place in their grids

- Allowing pupils to play as a pair or even a team

- Displaying a less than perfect example for pupils to critique and debate. This led one pupil to comment, 'Miss, shouldn't a bird house have a perch for the bird to sit on? This one doesn't'.

A WORD ABOUT MATHS

A comment I often hear is that success criteria are not needed in maths, however I would strongly dispute this. Many pupils find maths difficult and they can be supported enormously by having access to success criteria that break down the mathematical process into sequential steps. The example in Table 5.1 also features images which take away any ambiguity and allow pupils to see at a glance what is expected of them.

To summarise, the more energy and time we devote to success criteria, the easier and more effective marking becomes. You may wish to reflect on the following individually or with your colleagues.

Thinking about your current practice:

- Do you routinely share success criteria with your pupils?

- What form does this take?

- How engaged are the pupils with these criteria?

- How might we make the success criteria more engaging still?

Table 5.1   Breaking down the mathematical process into sequential steps to success (success criteria)

	What do I need to do?	Picture prompt	Self/peer feedback	Teacher feedback
1	Use a ruler			
2	Draw and label x and y axes			
3	Use an equally spaced scale			
4	Along the corridor then up the stairs			
5	Plot the coordinate on the line			
6	Use brackets and a comma when describing positions			

NOTE IT DOWN

HAVE A GO AT COMPLETING THE BLANK GRID BELOW.
THINK ABOUT A TOPIC YOU WILL BE TEACHING SOON
AND TRY TO IDENTIFY UP TO SIX OF THE MOST IMPORTANT
CRITERIA/INGREDIENTS. NEXT, THINK OF AN ICON OR IMAGE
THAT WILL DUAL-CODE THE CONCEPT AND MAKE IT MORE
MEMORABLE.

TRY THE GRID OUT WITH YOUR CLASS AS SOON AS YOU CAN
WHILST THE IDEAS ARE FRESH. REMEMBER TO ENGAGE THE
PUPILS WITH THE CO-CONSTRUCTION PROCESS, USING SOME
OF THE ACTIVITIES FROM THIS CHAPTER.

Table 5.2 Grid for listing success criteria and associated images

Criteria	Image	Peer/ self-assessed	Teacher assessed
1.			
2.			

Criteria	Image	Peer/ self-assessed	Teacher assessed
3.			
4.			
5.			
6.			

CHAPTER 6
WHAT IS THE
POINT ANYWAY?

In this chapter, we will explore:

- What to do with messages gleaned from marking
- How every teacher can be more effective in responding to assessment messages
- How to get started with making changes to your own practice.

REFLECTION

As you have worked your way through this book, hopefully you will have identified several practical strategies that could make your life easier when it comes to marking.

Take a moment to note down those ones that fit best with your teaching style and philosophy.

....

....

....

....

Whichever strategies you selected, we will now consider the most important question: what do we do with the messages gleaned from our marking? We need to shift marking from being simply an administrative task to being an analytical and diagnostic one. Quick tweaks to existing practice can help to ensure that all feedback generates formative data for the teachers, leading, in turn, to improvement actions for the learners.

ARE YOU A 'RESPONSIVE' TEACHER?

> 'Example of really big mistake? Calling
> Formative assessment Formative assessment rather
> than something like "responsive teaching".'
> Dylan Wiliam on Twitter, 23 October 2013

There is nothing new about formative assessment, or assessment for learning, which is defined as being 'part of everyday practice by students, teachers and peers that seeks, reflects upon and responds to information from dialogue, demonstration and observation in ways that enhance ongoing learning' (Conference participants, 2009: 2).

 # REFLECTION

This is rather harder in practice than it sounds in theory. Take a moment to reflect on the three verbs lurking in the middle of the definition: to *seek, reflect* and *respond*. Thinking about your own practice and your particular school, how much time do you devote to these various actions:

- **Seeking data?**
- **Reflecting on data?**
- **Responding to data?**

Many teachers agree that the current accountability culture means that they are spending a lot of time seeking and inputting data into various tracking systems, meaning they have less time for reflecting and responding. However, it is these actions that are the most vital. Dylan Wiliam's phrase 'responsive teaching' (on Twitter, 23 October 2013) reminds us of the dynamic action that needs to occur as the result of any assessment. Put simply, effective use of assessment improves teaching and learning.

 # HINTS & TIPS

Data can feel overwhelming at times and become a source of stress in itself. I have lost countless hours of my life trying to interpret various graphs and tables – in fact, I can feel my blood pressure rising even as I think about it!

(Continued)

If this is an area where you feel less confident, be assured that all you need is one method that allows you to quickly see how your pupils are doing.

Although there are many slick and impressive software packages that can perform diagnostic analysis for you, you don't necessarily need them. Periodically pause just to review and physically highlight the KPIs (key performance indicators) or AOs (assessment objectives) in your mark book or on screen using a RAG (red, amber, green) rating. The purpose here is to try to generate curricular targets by first identifying precisely what your class, groups or even individual pupils are finding most difficult. Subsequent teaching can then focus on directly addressing these.

It is worth reminding ourselves that data is always most powerful in the hands of the classroom teacher. A report from the University of Southampton back in 2010 coined the term 'data dictatorship and data democracy' (Kelly et al., 2010) and argued that, at that time, there was a 'clear hierarchy of data use within schools' (p.38), with the responsibility for managing data lying overwhelmingly with senior leaders. Data norms have changed over the last decade and I suspect that many schools would now consider themselves to be more democratic in terms of data usage.

For classroom teachers, often it is the qualitative, 'softer' elements of data that prove most useful. For example, what can we infer about the confidence of our pupils as they tackle a task? Pupils' hesitation in answering questions, or their willingness to attempt challenging work, are hugely revealing and may signal to the teacher the need to adapt the lesson and resources accordingly.

In summary, by being both responsive and adaptable, teachers can tailor their teaching more accurately to the needs of their pupils, especially when these responses are as immediate as possible. The following strategies are designed to help teachers respond to marking and other assessment messages immediately *within* the lesson rather than later.

STRATEGIES FOR THE CLASSROOM

- **Change what you are doing** – as any early years specialist will tell you, observation is one of the most important and intuitive tools of assessment. As soon as we notice that pupils are struggling, that is the signal to change what we are doing as teachers. As brilliant as the lesson plan itself may be, we must have the confidence to deviate from it when necessary. Dylan Wiliam argues that 'coverage is the enemy of learning' (on Twitter, 28 March 2018) so, rather than ploughing through content that is confusing, we need to pause and alter what happens next in that lesson.

Four of the most effective teacher feedback actions are:

  o **R**epeat

  o **R**eteach

  o **R**educe (simplify the task)

  o **R**egroup, e.g. work with smaller groups or allow peers to 'teach' each other.

- **Formative marking during the lesson** – make maximum use of the numbered success criteria grids (see Chapter 5) by circulating during pupils' independent work in class and annotating the grids in pencil as needed. If you find yourself making pencil marks against the same success criteria in multiple pieces of work, that should signal the need for a mini plenary, recap or reteach. For example, 'OK, pens down everybody. I notice from moving around and looking at your books that there seems to be an issue with success criterion number 4. Let's have another look at that together on the board'.

- **Small-group in-class intervention** is a particularly effective way to differentiate according to the specific criteria that pupils may be struggling with. Whilst guided (small-group work) is common in primary schools, it tends to be less established in the secondary sector, but it remains profoundly useful. We can support small groups of pupils in a more precise way than we can when trying to transmit to the whole class. For example, 'If you are finding criterion number 3 difficult, come to the front desk now and I will go through that again with you. I will be doing number 4 in 10 minutes' time'.

TAKE AWAY THE GUESS WORK: GET THE PUPILS TO TELL YOU

It was John Hattie (2011) who found that feedback ranked in the top 10 effect sizes, but one of his key findings was the fact that the most useful and important feedback of all is not that which the teacher gives to the pupils but, rather, that which is given by the pupils to their teacher. Are we providing ample opportunities for pupils to provide such feedback and, more importantly, how are we responding to the feedback that we do receive?

*   **Voting fingers** – take a mini plenary during the lesson and ask pupils to use their fingers to signal which of the success criteria they are finding the most challenging. Use the final section of the lesson to deliver a plenary in which you explicitly address the issue in the criterion that pupils have identified as being most challenging.

 CASE STUDY

IMPROVING THE USE OF EXIT CARDS

In our school, exit cards were used by many teachers to collect feedback from their pupils, often at the end of the school day. People used different formats, such as a question to answer (e.g. What did you find most challenging/fulfilling today?) or a simple sticky note for pupils to record their general thoughts and feelings about their learning.

Whilst these worked to a degree, we found that too much narrative detail in the pupils' responses made them a bit 'fluffy'.

It was really time-consuming for the teachers to process these and they actually gave us very little precise information that we could use. In the end, it felt like we were just doing it for the sake of it.

Instead, we decided to simplify things by asking pupils to just write down the numbers of up to two success criteria they were finding most difficult. Because there was no lengthy writing involved, this was quickly and easily completed and gave us an immediate sense of which *specific* things most pupils were struggling with. We could literally see this at a glance – especially when pupils handed their notes to us as they left the classroom.

As a result of this, we became much better at addressing these tricky areas in the next lesson. Everyone – including the pupils – now thinks that exit cards are useful and important.

To conclude, effective marking and feedback should serve a fundamental purpose: to identify where pupils are now, signpost where they should go next and show them how to get there. The challenge for the busy teacher is to step away from engrained marking habits that may be time-consuming but not necessarily effective and, instead, to focus their efforts on responding to feedback findings live in the classroom. Ultimately, there is little point in devoting time to any kind of marking if we do not intend to address the issues that it raises for us.

NOTE IT DOWN

The great news is, that by reducing the amount of time we spend marking, we can create space for other vital activities that will make us even more effective and efficient. Use the audit grid in Table 6.1 to reflect on your own practice. Identify one or two aspects that you may like to develop next.

Table 6.1 Grid for listing elements of practice reflected upon

Element of your practice	Always	Often	Sometimes	Rarely	Never
Gathering feedback from your pupils					
Simplifying the form in which pupils provide feedback, e.g. linked to the numbered success criteria					
Responding directly to pupils' feedback					
Small group interventions within the lesson					
Other					

REFERENCES

Beere, J. (2012) *The Perfect (Ofsted) Lesson*. Carmarthen: Independent Thinking Press.

Berger, R. (2003) *An Ethic of Excellence: Building a Culture of Craftsmanship with Students*. Portland, OR: Heinemann.

Brooks, V., Abbott, A. and Huddleston, P. (2004*) Preparing to Teach in Secondary Schools*. Maidenhead: Open University Press.

Bulger, M.E., Mayer, R., Almeroth, K. and Blau, S. (2008) 'Measuring learner engagement in computer-equipped college classrooms', *Journal of Educational Multimedia and Hypermedia*, 17(2): 129–43.

Butterfield, B. and Metcalfe, J. (2001) 'Errors committed with high confidence are hypercorrected', *Journal of Experimental Psychology: Learning, Memory and Cognition*, 27: 1491–4.

Conference participants (2009) Position Paper on Assessment for Learning. Paper presented at the Third International Conference on Assessment for Learning, Dunedin, New Zealand, March. Available at: www.fairtest.org/sites/default/files/Assess-for-Learning-position-paper.pdf (accessed 28 June 2020).

Doman, G. and Doman, J. (2006) *How to Teach Your Baby Math*. New York: Square One Publishing.

Elliott, V., Baird, J., Hopfenbeck, T., Ingram, J., Thompson, I., Usher, N., Zantout, M., Richardson, J. and Coleman, R. (2016) *A Marked Improvement? A Review of the Evidence on Written Marking*. Oxford: University of Oxford and Education Endowment Foundation (EEF).

Hattie, J. (2011) *Visible Learning for Teachers: Maximizing Impact on Learning*. Abingdon: Routledge.

Hattie, J., Frey, N. and Fisher, D. (2018) *Developing Assessment-Capable Visible Learners, Grades K-12: Maximizing Skill, Will, and Thrill*. Thousand Oaks, CA: Corwin.

Hendrick, C. Chronotope blog https://chronotopeblog.com/2017/09/02/four-quarters-marking-a-workload-solution/ (accessed 6 July 2020).

Hendrick, C. and Macpherson, R. (2017) *What Does This Look Like in the Classroom? Bridging the Gap Between Research and Practice*. Woodbridge: John Cat Educational Ltd.

Independent Teacher Workload Review Group (ITWRG) (2016) Eliminating unnecessary workload around marking: Report of the Independent Teacher Workload Review Group, March. Available at: https://assets.publishing.service.gov.uk/government/uploads/system/uploads/attachment_data/file/511256/Eliminating-unnecessary-workload-around-marking.pdf (accessed 28 June 2020).

Jones, J. (2011) *The Magic-Weaving Business: Finding the Heart of Learning and Teaching*. Oxford: Leannta Publishing.

Kelly, A., Downey, C. and Rietdijk, W. (2010) *Data Dictatorship and Data Democracy: Understanding Professional Attitudes to the Use of Pupil Performance Data in Schools.* Reading: CfBT Education Trust.

Kluger, A.N. and DeNisi, A. (1996) 'The effects of feedback interventions on performance: A historical review, a meta-analysis, and a preliminary feedback intervention theory', *Psychological Bulletin, 119*(2): 254–84.

Leahy, S., Lyon, C., Thompson, M. and Wiliam, D. (2005) Classroom assessment: Minute by minute, day by day, *Educational Leadership*, 63(3): 9–24.

Available at: www.ascd.org/publications/educational-leadership/nov05/vol63/num03/Classroom-Assessment@-Minute-by-Minute,-Day-by-Day.aspx (accessed 19 August 2020).

Paivio, A. (1971) *Imagery and Verbal Processes*. New York: Holt, Rinehart & Winston. (Republished in 1979 – Hillsdale, NJ: Erlbaum.)

Reinholz, D. (2016) 'The assessment cycle: A model for learning through peer assessment', *Assessment & Evaluation in Higher Education*, 41(2): 301–15.

Stiggins, R., Arter, J., Chappuis, J. and Chappuis, S. (2004) *Classroom Assessment for Student Learning: Doing it Right, Using it Well*. Portland, OR: Assessment Training Institute.

Sutton, R.M., Hornsey, M.J. and Douglas, K.M. (2011) *Feedback: The Communication of Praise, Criticism, and Advice*. Oxford: Peter Lang Publishing Inc.

Tyng, C., Amin, H. and Sad, N. (2017) 'The influences of emotion on learning and memory', *Frontiers in Psychology*, 8(1454): 1–22.

Wiliam, D. (2011) *Embedded Formative Assessment: Practical Strategies and Tools for K-12 Teachers*. Bloomington, IN: Solution Tree.

Walker, M., Worth, J. and Van den Brande, J. (2019) *Teacher Workload Survey 2019: Research Report*. Ref: DFE RR951. London: National Foundation for Educational Research (NFER) and Department for Education (DfE).

INDEX